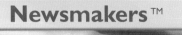

Newsmakers™

Ehud
Olmert

Prime Minister of
Israel

Michael A. Sommers

ROSEN
PUBLISHING®

New York

Glen Burnie H. S. Media Center

To ALS—for all your contributions

Published in 2008 by The Rosen Publishing Group, Inc.
29 East 21st Street, New York, NY 10010

Copyright © 2008 by The Rosen Publishing Group, Inc.

First Edition

Library of Congress Cataloging-in-Publication Data

Sommers, Michael A., 1966–
Ehud Olmert / Michael A. Sommers.—1st ed.
    p. cm.—(Newsmakers)
ISBN-13: 978-1-4042-1904-5
ISBN-10: 1-4042-1904-8
1. Olmert, Ehud, 1945– 2. Likud (Political party: Israel)—Biography—Juvenile literature. 3. Prime ministers—Israel—Biography—Juvenile literature. 4. Israel—Politics and government—Biography.
I. Title.
DS126.6.O44S66 2007
956.9405'4092—dc22
[B]
                                                            2006101202

Manufactured in the United States of America

On the cover: Foreground: In a speech on November 27, 2006, during a ceremony honoring Israel's first prime minister, David Ben-Gurion, Israeli prime minister Ehud Olmert offers the Palestinian people land in exchange for peace. Background: The city of Jerusalem.

CONTENTS

INTRODUCTION

On the evening of January 5, 2006, sixty-year-old Ehud Olmert was thrust onto the world stage when he suddenly became acting prime minister of Israel. Shortly after Prime Minister Ariel Sharon had a massive stroke and fell into a coma, Olmert, who was Sharon's deputy minister, received a phone call from the secretary of Sharon's cabinet, informing him of his new duties.

Nobody, least of all Olmert, had expected that Sharon would suffer such a fate. Two weeks earlier, on the morning of December 18, 2005,

Deputy Prime Minister Ehud Olmert whispers to Prime Minister Ariel Sharon during a session of the Knesset (Israel's parliament) in October 2004.

Olmert was just about to leave for his gym when he received a phone call from the director of a hospital telling him that the prime minister had been admitted and needed to undergo surgery to seal a small hole in his heart. Later, however, he received news that Sharon's condition wasn't as serious as was initially believed. The operation didn't need to be performed right away. After a few days spent under observation in the hospital, Sharon returned to work and continued to perform his duties.

In fact, on January 4, 2006, both Ariel Sharon and Ehud Olmert were at the prime minister's office. That afternoon, Sharon's secretary asked Olmert to speak with the prime minister in his private chambers. He entered the room of his colleague and mentor, whom he had known for over thirty years. Sharon told him that the following day, he would go into the hospital, where he would undergo a three-hour surgery. During this time, said Sharon, Olmert would take over all prime minister duties. In a 2006 PBS *Frontline* documentary called "The Unexpected Candidate," Olmert speaks of this moment to Israeli journalist/producer Ofra Bikel, a friend of the Olmert family. He remembers that he joked about stepping into his friend's shoes, telling Sharon, "I made up my mind, I'm not going to make any major decisions tomorrow in the three hours," and saying, "Except for one." When Sharon asked what that was, Olmert responded,

"I want to replace your staff," which caused Sharon to break into laughter.

After discussing some political matters, Olmert said, "I'm already waiting to hear your voice calling me after these three hours telling me, 'Ehud, I relieve you of the responsibility of prime minister.'" His final words before hugging Sharon good-bye were, "This country needs you. Come back." In the documentary, Olmert recalls that the exchange was an emotional experience for both of them. Indeed, Sharon's cabinet secretary, who was present, has said that every time he recalls their farewell, he begins to cry. At the time, however, never for a moment did Olmert believe that several hours later Sharon would suffer a major stroke and that they would never again speak to each other.

When Olmert received the tragic news later that evening, he was having dinner in a restaurant with his wife, Aliza, and several American friends. Shortly afterward, he and Aliza left the restaurant. When they arrived home, Sharon's cabinet secretary called him to say that the attorney general was on the line and that the call was being taped. Olmert knew that the attorney general's words—that, as of that moment, Olmert possessed the authority of the prime minister of Israel—would constitute an official act.

Ehud Olmert was aware that his life, and that of his family, as well as his country, had changed, perhaps forever. Said Olmert of that moment: "This was the end of an era. The end of one of the most dramatic periods in the life of our country and perhaps a new beginning, and maybe, hopefully, I will be the one that has to take this country into this new beginning. And, naturally, that means that life will never be the same for me."

CHAPTER ONE

BEGINNINGS

E hud Olmert was born on September 30, 1945, in the Jewish settlement of Binyamina. Today, the town, which is famous for its production of honey and wine, is located in northern Israel, south of the city of Haifa. But when Olmert was born, the nation of Israel didn't exist. It was but a dream for many Jewish people.

Binyamina lay within a region of the Middle East known as the British Protectorate of Palestine. This was a territory made up of what today is Jordan and Israel. Before World War I, the Ottoman Turkish Empire controlled this area. But during the war, British forces occupied Palestine and began to govern the region. By the end of World War I, the Ottoman Empire had crumbled and the League of Nations (the predecessor of today's United Nations) gave the territory to Great Britain to administer on a permanent basis.

This nineteenth-century engraving by British painter David Roberts (1796–1864) depicts Jerusalem, the Holy City. The Temple Mount, with the Dome of the Rock, can be seen in the background.

THE PROMISED LAND

At the time, Palestine was home to Arabs as well as an increasing number of Jews, who had been settling in the region for hundreds of years. According to Jewish tradition, the land of

Israel had been a Jewish holy land and the Promised Land for 3,000 years. Judaism's most important religious sites—including remains of the second temple completed by Jewish king Herod—were located there, in the holy city of Jerusalem. Beginning in the eleventh century BCE, for 1,000 years, the region had been ruled by a series of Jewish kingdoms. Then a gradual succession of invaders, including the Babylonians, Persians, and Greeks, conquered the area and put pressure on the Jews who lived there to leave. In 132 CE, a Roman invasion forced the largest expulsion of the Jews. Under Roman rule, in an attempt to erase Jewish ties to the land, the region's name was changed to Syria Palaestina. Yet, some Jews still remained in the region. They continued to live there even when Muslims conquered the region in 638 CE. For centuries afterward, Jews living in Europe and other parts of the world continued to think of Palestine as their traditional holy land. Over time, waves of Jews, who in many countries were persecuted due to their religion, immigrated back to the Middle East, creating Jewish settlements.

In the nineteenth century, a political movement known as Zionism was growing in popularity among Jews. Zionism supports a traditional homeland for the Jewish people in the Land of Israel. It is partially based on religious tradition set out in the Hebrew Bible (the Old Testament), which talks about the Israelites, or Jews, and their relationship with God. The Bible referred to Jacob—who later took the name Israel—as the father of all Israelites and told the tale of how God led them from Egypt to the Land of Israel. According to the Bible, it was Solomon, king of the Jews, who built the first permanent Jewish temple in the city of Jerusalem.

Zionism also spread through Europe as a result of the rise of anti-Semitism in many European countries. As Zionism gathered support, more and more Jews began returning to their historic homeland, Palestine, where they hoped they would be safe. These increasing waves of immigrants, who occupied land and started farming communities, caused the region's Arab inhabitants, most of whom were Muslims, to feel threatened. The Muslims also considered the region of Palestine—and the city of Jerusalem with its holy Muslim sites—to be their holy land.

Therefore, by 1923, when the British took over administration of Palestine, land conflicts already existed between Jews and Muslims. However, the British made two promises to the people living there. First, in return for their support during World War I, they promised the local Arabs independence for a united Arab country. Second, the British promised to create and support a Jewish national homeland in the region. They emphasized that this new state would not harm the civil and religious rights of existing non-Jewish communities in Palestine. At the time, the majority of Palestine's inhabitants were Arabic-speaking Muslims, while about 11 percent were Hebrew-speaking Jews. Unfortunately, the British didn't follow through on their promises. As a result, Arabs and Jews grew increasingly frustrated and began pressuring the British authorities.

MIGRATIONS

Ehud Olmert's parents were among the many Jewish Zionists who came to Palestine in the early twentieth century. After World War I, Olmert's father, Mordechai (then a boy), and his family had escaped persecution in war-torn Russia and fled to the Chinese city of Harbin, which was the largest Jewish center in the Far East. When he was sixteen, Mordechai was one of the founders of Harbin's local Betar youth group. Betar—whose name refers to an ancient battle site—was a Zionist movement that supported fighting for a national homeland in Israel. In Harbin, Mordechai met a young woman named Bella Vugmann, whose family had emigrated from the Ukraine. A dedicated Betar activist, Bella would become his lifelong companion and his wife.

In 1930, the newly married couple left China for Holland, where Mordechai studied agriculture. Their real dream, however, was to help build a Jewish state where they could live peacefully in

In 1909, Zionist settlers gather in the desert of Turkish-ruled Palestine to decide where to build what would eventually become the region's first all-Jewish city in 2,000 years. The settlers named the city Tel Aviv, meaning "Hill of Spring."

the land of their ancestors. Mordechai was twenty-two in 1933, the year he and Bella arrived in Palestine. He purchased land, and the couple began farming. Mordechai also became one of the pioneers of Israel's land settlement and a fierce fighter for a Jewish nation. In Palestine, many

Background: Settling the Land

Even before Israel existed as a nation, Jews who migrated to their ancient homeland sought to ensure Jewish existence in the Middle East by buying or occupying land and building communities known as settlements. More recently, they sought to sink their roots into the soil by building housing projects and defending every hill, plain, and valley in order to prove to other Israelis—and their Arab enemies—that Jews were there to stay no matter what. Throughout Israel's history, encouraging settlers would become a major policy for the government and a key source of conflict between Israelis and Arabs, not to mention between Israelis themselves.

As Ehud Olmert explained in an interview for the *Frontline* documentary "The Unexpected Candidate," "You must understand that for us Israelis ... settlements were the purest form of the realization of the Zionist ethos [ideology]. When Jews came to this part of the world in the 1860s and on ... what did they do here in those old days? They built settlements, and settlements are what made Israel, eventually, into what it was."

members of the Betar movement, Mordechai Olmert included, fought against the British as part of an underground military group known as the Irgun. (Menachem Begin, a Zionist of Lithuanian origin, led the group.) Radical Zionists, the Irgun attacked the British authorities and Arabs in Palestine throughout the 1930s and some of the 1940s, believing that only force could guarantee the Jews a right to a homeland. Many Jews, moderate Zionists, Arabs, and British considered the Irgun to be violent terrorists. However, Irgun members considered their actions necessary against Arab attacks on Jewish settlers and against British authorities, who restricted entrance of Jewish immigrants to Palestine. Despite these limitations, by 1940, Jews made up 30 percent of the population of Palestine, and Zionist organizations had purchased vast tracts of land from the Arabs and British.

Jewish immigrants trying to get to Palestine multiplied during World War II. This was a result of Adolf Hitler and his anti-Semitic Nazi regime: Jews in German-occupied territories through-out Europe were hunted down and sent to concentration camps, where many were cruelly tortured and murdered. European Jews fled these horrors and sought refuge in droves. Determined to save lives, Jewish groups such as the Irgun helped smuggle in Jewish refugees and resorted to escalating violence when they were met with resistance from Palestinian Arabs and British authorities.

This was the environment into which Ehud Olmert was born. In fact, until he was two, his family lived in an old Turkish fortress near the Mediterranean coast. Although disguised as an agricultural settlement, in reality, the Irgun used the complex to train secretly its underground fighters.

BIRTH OF THE STATE OF ISRAEL

Tired of the increasing violence, at the end of World War II, Britain decided it wanted to stop its administration of Palestine, leaving the newly formed United Nations (UN) with the task of solving the growing conflicts between Palestine's Arabs and Jews. In 1947, the UN decided to honor Britain's original promise to both Arabs and Jews by dividing Palestine into two independent states, with the city of Jerusalem placed under international administration to avoid conflict. Arabs would receive 45 percent of Palestinian territory, while Jews would receive the other 55 percent. Reaction to the UN plan couldn't have been more divided. Arabs in Palestine and throughout much of the Middle East rejected the UN's proposal. So did a few Jews, including members of the Irgun, who were angered at having foreign powers divide up what they considered to be their Jewish homeland. However, the majority of Palestine's Jewish population was overjoyed.

Nonetheless, it was no surprise that when the UN plan became law on November 29, 1947, fighting broke out between Arabs and Israelis, sparking what would become the 1948 Israeli War of Independence. The day before the British pulled out of Palestine on May 15, 1948, the State of Israel became official. No sooner had Israel been established than neighboring armies of Egypt, Syria, Jordan, Lebanon, and Iraq joined Arab Palestinians in their escalating war against the young Israeli nation. It was during this time that Israel's national military, known as the Israeli Defense Forces (IDF) came into being.

After months of fighting, a cease-fire was declared in 1949 and temporary borders were drawn between Israel and its neighbors. This frontier was known as the Green Line since during peace talks the new borders were drawn on a map using a green pencil. Although Israel had gained an extra 25 percent of former British Palestine territory, Jordan controlled the mountainous region along the Jordan River known as the West Bank, and Egypt took possession of the Gaza Strip, a small strip of land along the Mediterranean coast. The city of Jerusalem was divided, with Jordan taking the eastern parts, including the Old City, and Israel taking the western parts.

Following the war, large numbers of Arabs fled from the newly created Jewish state. Although Israel offered Arab inhabitants "full and equal citizenship," many Arabs refused to stay. Ongoing immigration of Jewish refugees from Europe, however, caused Israel's population to double within a year. Meanwhile, Israel's first prime minister, David Ben-Gurion, set about the enormous task of building a stable new nation.

OUTSIDERS

One of Ben-Gurion's goals was to ban underground military organizations such as the Irgun, which were classified as terrorists groups. By 1949, the Olmert family, which included three-year-old Ehud and two older brothers, moved out of the old Turkish fortress and into another agricultural settlement. Along with other former Irgun members, they built homes close together in a closed-off neighborhood of Binyamina that they named Nahalat Jabotinsky, after a famous Zionist leader. With the Irgun outlawed, many of its members, including the Olmerts, joined a right-wing, nationalist, radical Zionist party created by Menachem Begin, called Herut (the Hebrew word for "freedom").

Herut was initially a small political party, but it managed to elect fourteen representatives to the Knesset, or Israeli assembly, following Israel's

This portrait of Ehud Olmert's father, Mordechai, was taken in 1959, when he was elected for the second time to the Knesset as a member of Herut.

first democratic elections in January 1949. The major party, which formed Israel's first government, was the Mapai, or the Israeli Workers' Party. This socialist party was more left-wing than Herut and was comprised of more moderate Zionists led by David Ben-Gurion. For decades, the Workers' Party, which would later become the Labor Party, would head the Israeli government, with Herut as the opposition party. In fact, in its early years, Herut was viewed as an extremist party of outsiders and its members often suffered discrimination. In the 1950s, Mordechai Olmert was elected twice (in 1955 and 1959) to the Knesset as a Herut member. However, both Mordechai and Bella were independent thinkers. When, over time, Mordechai refused to agree with all of Herut's views, he was ultimately rejected from the party. As such, the Olmerts became outsiders within a community of outsiders.

Ehud and his brothers (his parents would have one more son, Yossi, in 1949) had a rigid upbringing. Bella, in particular, was strict and expected a lot from her sons. She also encouraged them to do their best. It was she who kept on top of young Ehud to practice piano and do his homework. Meanwhile, like his other brothers, Ehud was a high achiever at school, excelling in both academic subjects and sports. Early on, he developed a great passion for soccer.

In the Olmert home, aside from Hebrew, Mordechai and Bella spoke Chinese to each other, especially when they didn't want their children to overhear the political topics they were discussing. Meanwhile, like his parents before him, Ehud joined the local Betar youth movement as a teenager. Growing up, he couldn't help but be influenced by the strong Zionist views of his parents and their commitment to a Jewish state.

In fact, he was raised to believe that part of the country belonged to Jews. It had been taken by Arabs and was still ruled by Arabs, but one day it would be freed and returned to the Israelis— by force, if necessary. Ultimately, his parents' beliefs would greatly influence Ehud's political career. As well, their independent spirit would give him the strength to differ repeatedly in opinion from the majority.

CHAPTER TWO

THE SIX-DAY WAR

A side from a 1956 conflict known as the Suez Crisis, in which Israel, France, and Britain invaded Egypt when the latter prohibited them from access to the Suez Canal, the years between 1956 and 1966 were a time of relative peace between Israel and its Arab neighbors. During this time, the Israeli Defense Forces (IDF) developed from an improvised army into a professional fighting force with an impressive arsenal of modern arms and weapons.

MILITARY

From the time of Israel's founding, it was considered essential that all Israeli citizens be trained and prepared to defend their people and nation from any threat. Young Israeli men were required to serve three years in the military, and young women generally served two years. In November 1963, at the age of eighteen, Ehud Olmert began his compulsory military service

From inside a tank on January 1, 1975, a soldier from the Israeli Defense Forces (IDF) prepares his gun for action.

with the IDF. He spent his time as an infantry unit officer in the 13th Regiment of the legendary Golani Brigade, whose officers were reputed for their courage, toughness, and ability to think fast.

Ehud dreamed of a great military career. However, early on in his service, while doing training exercises, he broke an arm and a leg, and subsequently spent months receiving medical treatment. During his recuperation, he decided to enroll at the Hebrew University of Jerusalem, where he majored in philosophy and psychology while continuing his political activism and his involvement in Herut.

Intelligent and ambitious, Ehud was only twenty when he made a name for himself as a member of Herut. In the first of many memorable public speeches, he shocked the audience by standing up at a party meeting and demanding the resignation of Herut's leader, Menachem Begin. (Ehud blamed him for Herut having lost a series of government elections.) Party members were outraged. Begin was considered an untouchable hero who shouldn't be criticized, especially by a young upstart. Members of the crowd stormed the podium where Ehud stood and would have physically attacked him if Begin himself had not stopped them, insisting that Ehud Olmert complete his speech.

ALIZA

At Hebrew University, Ehud met an attractive, intelligent psychology student named Aliza Richter.

The daughter of German Holocaust survivors who had escaped Germany and came to Israel after World War II, Aliza was born in a refugee camp for German Jews. Like the Olmerts, the Richter family was quite poor. However, they weren't national activists like the Olmerts. When Aliza's parents arrived in Israel, they had nothing. All they wanted was a safe refuge where they could start a new life without suffering persecution as a minority group. Growing up, Aliza was taught to be thankful for the little she had and that it was important to share whatever she had to take care of those who had even less than she did. These "socialist" ideas had a profound influence on Aliza and later led her to becoming a political activist, like Ehud. However, while Ehud was concerned with fighting for nationalist causes, Aliza was involved in concerns such as creating a more equal society.

Ehud was immediately interested in Aliza. Initially, however, the feeling wasn't mutual. Having heard his public speeches, Aliza found Ehud to be arrogant and aggressive. Because of this, she wouldn't go on a date with him. Ehud was undeterred. Aliza worked part-time as a waitress, and Ehud convinced the restaurant's manager to give him Aliza's phone number. Over the course of multiple phone calls, Aliza discovered that Ehud had a more charming private side, and she finally agreed to go out with him. Despite their radically different backgrounds and political views, the two fell in love. Said Aliza, in a recent interview cited by Thomas O'Dwyer in the *Guardian*, "A boy meets a girl, a girl meets a boy, and that's the whole story. You don't talk ideology in those special moments." Indeed, after only three days, the modern-day Israeli version of Romeo and Juliet informed their stunned families that they were getting married.

THE SIX-DAY WAR

As a young man, Ehud Olmert's earliest political mentor was a charismatic, talented lawyer named Shmuel Tamir. Before Israeli independence, Tamir had been chief of intelligence of the Irgun and had been involved in operations against British authorities. In fact, he was so feared by the British that they sent him into exile in Africa. When he returned to the new State of Israel, he became a prominent member of Herut and was elected to the Knesset in 1965. In 1967, however, he broke with Menachem Begin and formed the Free Center Party, taking Olmert along with him. Only a few months later, the situation in Israel and the entire Middle East changed forever when the Six-Day War began.

From its creation in 1948, Israel continued to have difficult relations with its Arab neighbors. All Arab states refused to recognize Israel as an independent state. Over the years, armed conflicts—notably the Suez Crisis of 1956—broke out along the shared borders between Israel and Egypt, Syria, and Jordan. In fact, Israel believed that it was only a matter of time before these nations mounted a massive attack against it.

Following the Suez Crisis, UN peacekeeping forces moved in to patrol sensitive border areas between Israel and its neighbors, and Israeli military troops were forced to withdraw from the Sinai Peninsula and the Gaza Strip.

The Suez Crisis

The Suez Canal is an important waterway that connects the Red Sea (in Asia) to the Mediterranean Sea (and Europe). A canal dug by ancient pharaohs was subsequently closed in the eighth century. The building of the modern canal began in the 1850s, after the ruler of Egypt—who controlled the surrounding territory—gave permission to the French-run Suez Canal Company. Completed in 1869, the canal was to allow free access to all nations.

In 1875, when Egypt sold its shares in the Suez Canal Company to Great Britain, England gained control of the canal. In 1951, however, Egypt refused to recognize Britain's rights over the canal and attempted to nationalize the Suez Canal Company, saying it rightfully belonged to Egypt. As a result, in 1956, Britain, France, and Israel—all of whom had important economic and trading interests in the canal—invaded Egypt. A week later, the United States convinced the three countries to withdraw. UN peacekeeping forces were sent to patrol the surrounding region of the Sinai Peninsula and the Gaza Strip, both of which were Egyptian territories. Since 1981, a multinational force of observers continues to monitor the canal and surrounding area.

As a result, for some time, relations between Israel and its neighbors were calm. However, the UN was only in the Middle East with the agreement of the nations where it had troops. In early May 1967, Egypt decided that it no longer wanted UN troops in the Suez region that marked its frontier with Israel. Instead, Egypt sent a large number of its own forces to patrol the border area. Shortly after, on May 23, the Egyptian government closed off the Straits of Tiran to all Israeli ships, which Israel claimed was illegal. Both events left Israel certain that Egypt was planning to attack. Instead of waiting to be invaded, Israel decided to take matters into its own hands.

This map of the Middle East shows Israel and its neighbors, Egypt, Jordan, Syria, and Lebanon. The circled area shows the Suez Canal and pinpoints the regions— the West Bank, Gaza Strip, and Golan Heights— occupied by Israeli forces as a result of the Six-Day War.

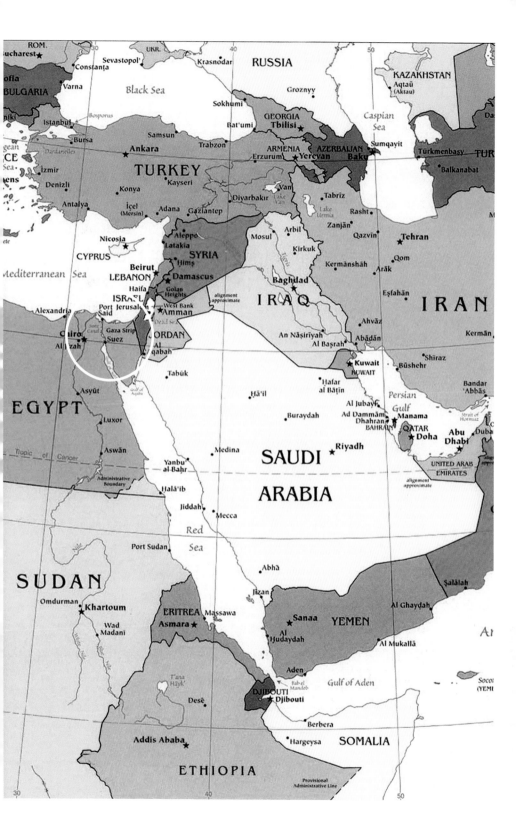

On June 5, Israel struck preemptively by launching an enormous military campaign against the countries it believed to be its enemies: Egypt, Syria, Jordan, and Iraq. At the time, Israel had the most sophisticated army and air force in the Middle East. All but 12 of its nearly 200 fighter jets were involved in a massive attack against Egypt's airfields on the morning of June 5. However, no one—not even the Israelis themselves—expected that on the first day of what would become known as the Six-Day War, Israel would wipe out practically the entire air force of Egypt. Next to Israel's, Egypt's air force was the largest and most powerful in the Middle East. Israel destroyed more than 300 of Egypt's 450 planes, along with most of its runways. During the next three days, Israel went on to defeat the lesser air forces of Jordan, Syria, and Iraq. After its air force had cleared the way, Israeli ground troops began their onslaught. On June 7, after having destroyed a large number of Egyptian tanks in the Sinai Desert, Israeli forces reached the Suez Canal. That same day, Israeli troops in Jordan had pushed back Jordanian forces from the entire West Bank of the Jordan River. To the north, from June 8 to 10, Israeli troops fought Syrian troops in the mountainous Golan Heights region. Not only did they capture the Heights, but they also advanced 30 miles (48 kilometers) into Syria itself. This was Israel's final offensive. The following day, on June 11, a cease-fire was signed between all nations.

The war was seen as a disaster for the Arab world. Not only was it a military catastrophe, it was a terrible blow to Arab pride. Four of the most powerful Arab nations had been defeated by one tiny country. Not even the Israelis had expected such an outcome. Their surprise quickly gave way to celebration. Yet, Israel's victory was ultimately bittersweet: it would plant the seed for enormous problems—that continue to this day—between the region's Jews and Arabs.

In capturing the Sinai Peninsula, Golan Heights, Gaza Strip, and West Bank of the Jordan River (including East Jerusalem), Israel

On June 5, 1967, the first day of the Six-Day War, Israeli tanks advance toward Egyptian troops near the town of Rafah, located along the Gaza Strip.

had succeeded in occupying regions of great strategic importance. Israel's territory had tripled, and it now had close to one million Arabs living directly under its control in the newly captured territories. However, the "occupied territories" would be a major source of conflict. Only Arab inhabitants of East Jerusalem and the Golan Heights were allowed to receive partial rights as Israeli residents (when Israel officially annexed these territories in the early 1980s). Perhaps the most troublesome occupied territory was the West Bank. Although many of the Arab Palestinians who lived there fled into neighboring Jordan, more than 600,000 remained and lived under Israeli administration. Unhappy with the way they were treated by Israeli authorities, many young Arabs organized themselves into small military groups that periodically revolted against Israeli soldiers who patrolled the areas.

Meanwhile, in order to secure a permanent foothold in these newly acquired territories, an Israeli settlement effort was launched. Jewish people moved into occupied territories, where they had lived for years prior to the founding of Israel. Hundreds of thousands of Jews began cultivating land, constructing houses, and setting down roots they hoped would be permanent.

The Six-Day War and Israel's occupation and subsequent settlement of the captured territories laid the foundation for future conflicts in the region. On November 22, 1967, the UN Security Council adopted Resolution 242. Known as the "land for peace" resolution, it called for Israel to withdraw "from territories occupied" in 1967 in return for "the termination of all claims or states of belligerency [aggression]." However, in response to Arab nations' refusal to accept Israel as a state, the UN resolution also under-lined the right of "every state in the area"—including Israel—"to live in peace within secure and recognized boundaries free from threats or acts of force."

CHAPTER THREE

THE KNESSET

E hud Olmert hadn't seen any military action during the Six-Day War. After completing his BA degree in psychology and philosophy in 1968, Olmert, fully recuperated from his earlier injuries, returned to complete his military service. Instead of being an officer, however, he worked as a journalist for the IDF's newspaper, *Hamahane*. During this time, the political party formed by his mentor, Shmuel Tamir, collapsed. Gradually, many of its members, including Olmert, made peace with Menachem Begin and joined his newly formed coalition party, Likud.

THE LIKUD

Likud—Hebrew for "consolidation"—was formed in the early 1970s. It brought together several parties from the right wing and center, including many from the former Herut and Tamir's Free Center Party. Most Likud members—including

Menachem Begin, Ariel Sharon (who contributed to the founding of the party), and Ehud Olmert—believed that the Zionist cause should manifest itself in retaining the territories captured during the 1967 war. Likud members supported Israeli occupation of the territories captured in the Six-Day War. In order to better defend the existence of Israel, they actively encouraged settlers to move into these areas, particularly the West Bank, while opposing Arab Palestinians' demand for their own independent state.

One of Likud's first goals was to win the national elections in 1973 against the center-left Labor Party, which had been in power since 1948. In its first decades of existence, the Labor Party—known until 1968 as Mapai—was a strong supporter of settlements both within Israel and some parts of the occupied territories captured in 1967. Over time, however, in the name of peace (and what they viewed as fairness to Palestinians), many of its members came to believe that Israeli settlers should leave the occupied territories, particularly the West Bank,

This photograph of Ehud Olmert was taken in 1974, one year after he was elected to the Knesset for the first time, as a member of Likud.

and return them to Palestinians. More recently, many Labor Party members have also supported Palestinians' right to their own independent state.

In spite of Likud's efforts, the Labor Party once again won the elections in 1973. Likud succeeded in winning thirty-nine seats in the Knesset, however. Among those who won a seat was Ehud Olmert, who at the age of twenty-eight became the youngest legislator in Israel's history.

THE CRUSADER

Still as outspoken as he had been in his university days, Olmert was known by colleagues as somewhat of a troublemaker and a crusader in search of justice. However, the first crusade he undertook was hardly a pressing political issue. Still a great soccer fan, Olmert was upset that Israel's professional soccer league was run by organized crime. He tried to bring this fact to the government's attention. However, with Israel still struggling to deal with its newly occupied territories, few members of the Knesset were willing to pay attention to Olmert's pleas on behalf of the integrity of soccer. In fact, as reported by Israeli professor and writer Gadi Taub in the *New Republic*, after Olmert presented his findings to the Knesset, the minister of the interior remarked: "In this country nothing is organized. What makes you think crime, of all things, would be?"

Unfazed by his colleagues' reactions, Olmert continued to investigate justice issues, but he began to focus on more serious ones within the Labor government. Working closely with journalists, Olmert uncovered the criminal connections of a military hero, General Rehavam Zeevy. He also exposed the corrupt dealings of Abraham Offer, the minister of housing. His revelations caused great embarrassment to the ruling Labor Party, and the investigations made national headlines. (Offer was ultimately acquitted, but not before he committed suicide.) To the Israeli public, Olmert became known as "the investigator member of Knesset."

Olmert's interest in crime and justice was professional as well as political. In the late 1960s, while honing his political skills, he had also decided to pursue a legal career. In 1970, he enrolled once again at Hebrew University in Jerusalem, where he spent the next three years earning a law degree. After he entered the Knesset, the attention he received from his political investigations also brought him legal clients, many of whom were members of Israel's wealthy and powerful elite. In 1975, he started practicing law at a private law firm, where he would become increasingly busy.

THE YOM KIPPUR WAR

Yom Kippur is the most important religious day of the Jewish calendar. It means "Day of Atonement" in Hebrew, and Jews traditionally spend the day praying and fasting. This is what the vast majority of Israelis were doing on Yom Kippur morning of October 6, 1973, when Egyptian and Syrian military forces, knowing that most Israeli Jews, including soldiers, would be involved in religious activities, launched a surprise attack.

Ever since the Six-Day War, both Egypt and Syria had been determined to secure—by any means possible—the return of the territories they had lost. When they finally attacked, Israeli forces were not only unprepared but also out-numbered. From the Golan Heights, 1,400 Syrian tanks faced down 150 Israeli tanks, while in the Sinai region, 500 Israeli soldiers found themselves face-to-face with 80,000 Egyptian soldiers. In addition, other Arab nations had lent their support to Egypt and Syria. Iraq sent fighter planes and 18,000 soldiers to the Golan Heights, and both Saudi Arabia and Jordan sent troops and money.

Taken completely by surprise, Israeli forces were quickly overwhelmed. Within two days,

Major General Ariel Sharon *(with bandaged head, at right)* of the Israeli army discusses strategies with General Haim Bar-Lev while studying a map of the Sinai Desert during the 1973 Yom Kippur War.

Egyptian troops had crossed the Suez Canal and advanced across the Sinai while Syrian troops made great headway across the Golan Heights. A crushing Israeli defeat appeared inevitable. However, on October 8, Israeli forces, strengthened by reserve fighters and led in part by a fearless young commander named Ariel Sharon, launched a counterattack in the Sinai. They succeeded in pushing Egyptian forces back across the Suez Canal and advanced within 65 miles (105 km) of Cairo, Egypt's capital. In the Golan Heights, the Israelis were also able to push back the Syrians. After recapturing the Heights, Israeli troops advanced upon Damascus, stopping only after they were within 35 miles (56 km) of the Syrian capital.

Two weeks later, on October 24, the United Nations persuaded the two sides to agree to a cease-fire and sent peacekeeping forces to patrol the still dangerous border regions between Israel and both Egypt and Syria. The Yom Kippur War once again proved the might of Israel's military forces. However, Israel's success was in large part due to the aid of its closest ally: the United States. Not only had America provided the IDF with sophisticated arms and weapons, but it also shared its intelligence with the Israelis. As a result, Israeli commanders knew exactly where enemy troops were located and could coordinate counterattacks.

Despite the fact that they had been taken by surprise and had experienced many casualties, Israel's seemingly miraculous victory boosted Israeli morale. Meanwhile, Arab nations, particularly Egypt, felt less humiliated than they had after the Six-Day War, even though they hadn't succeeded in regaining control of the Israeli-occupied territories. On a more personal level, the war brought together Ehud Olmert

While apartment residents watch, UN peacekeeping forces guard a settlement during the Yom Kippur War.

and Ariel Sharon, both of whom had been instrumental in the founding of Likud. When Sharon was stationed in the Sinai Peninsula, Ehud joined his headquarters, briefly resuming his duties as a military correspondent for the IDF's *Hamahane* newspaper.

Ultimately, the importance of the Yom Kippur War was that it marked a turning point in Israel-Arab relations. Prior to the war, Egyptian president Anwar Sadat had been a leader in the Arab world's opposition to Israel. His willingness to destroy Israel had made him a hero in the eyes of Israel's Arab Palestinian population. In fact, in the event of an Arab victory, he had promised the Palestinians and their leader, Yasir Arafat, control of the West Bank and Gaza Strip territories. After the Yom Kippur War, Sadat realized that war was not a solution and that Israel could not be defeated by military means.

In September 1975, with the diplomatic encouragement of the United States, Egypt and Israel signed a historic agreement in which they vowed to settle their differences through peaceful means. In 1979, after years of diplomatic talks, the nations signed the Israel-Egypt Peace Treaty. It was the first time any Arab nation had officially recognized Israel as a state. In return for lasting peace, Israel withdrew its troops and settlers from Egypt's Sinai territories.

The PLO

The Palestine Liberation Organization (PLO), a political and military group, was founded in 1964 by various Arab groups who defended the Arab Palestinians' right to their homeland of Palestine (including the land given to Israel by the United Nations). The organization's goal was to destroy the State of Israel—the creation of which many Arabs had never accepted—through military means. They dreamed of an independent Palestinian state that would stretch from the Jordan River to the Mediterranean Sea.

Following the crushing Arab defeat in the Six-Day War, the PLO became increasingly dominated by a Palestinian group called Fatah. Fatah was led by Yasir Arafat, an activist who became leader of the PLO in 1969. When Israel refused to surrender the Arab territories it had captured in 1967, the PLO began to organize violent revolts. Although Israel treated the PLO as a terrorist organization and sent the IDF to hunt down its leaders, most Arabs viewed the Palestinians as heroes fighting against oppressive Israeli settlers and troops for land that was rightfully theirs. In fact, in 1974, Arab leaders declared that the PLO would become the official representative for Palestine and all Palestinians at a national and international level.

Many Arabs felt that Sadat had betrayed them. In fact, his change of attitude toward Israel would cost him his life: Muslim fundamentalists assassinated him in 1981. Meanwhile, as Egypt and Israel initiated an era of peaceful diplomatic relations, some Palestinians, who were increasingly frustrated at living under Israeli rule, became more violent and extreme. They resorted to murders, suicide bombings, and terrorist attacks against Israeli civilians and military. Their aim was to force Israel to withdraw its troops and settlers from the West Bank and Gaza.

CHAPTER FOUR

MAYOR OF JERUSALEM

In May 1977, a historic event occurred in Israel. For the first time ever, the Labor Party, which had headed the government since 1948, was defeated in national elections by the right-wing opposition. Likud formed Israel's government, and its leader, Menachem Begin, became prime minister, a position he would hold until 1983.

THE OLMERT FAMILY

A member of Likud, Ehud Olmert was once again elected to the Knesset. He also began to enjoy professional success as a lawyer. In 1978, Olmert had opened his own law firm in Jerusalem, where he advised clients on multimillion-dollar real-estate transactions. Olmert, who was reputed to be a slick dealmaker, succeeded in earning a considerable amount of money over time. After years of moving from one rental apartment to another, Ehud and Aliza purchased a big house in an expensive neighborhood in Jerusalem. Since their marriage, the couple had had four children: Michal, Dana, Shaul, and Ariel, and had adopted a fifth, Shuli. As in most Israeli families, political subjects were frequent topics of discussion.

The differences between Ehud and Aliza remained. While Ehud was outgoing and dashing, Aliza was much more down-to-earth and discreet, favoring a life outside of the limelight. Politically, they continued to agree to disagree. Ehud supported Israel's use of military force to defend the occupied territories and encouraged Jewish settlements. Aliza favored diplomatic efforts to achieve peace and believed that the Palestinians had a right to their own land and state. At home, lively discussions sometimes gave way to heated arguments.

While raising their children, Aliza had also become a social worker, specializing in working with at-risk children. Highly creative, she later left social work to concentrate on becoming a writer and artist. (She continued to be active in social causes, particularly those with an impact on disadvantaged children.) Gradually, she gained national and international recognition for her work as a playwright, sculptor, and painter.

In 1981, 1984, and 1988, Olmert was successively reelected to the Knesset, and during these years, his political career began to take off. Along with several other promising young politicians (many of them children of Irgun commanders), he was known as one of "the Likud princes." He participated in many committees and served as minister of minority affairs (1988–1990) and minister of health (1990–1992). During this time, Israelis viewed Olmert as being quite right-wing. He had been one of the few Likud members to vote against Begin's 1979 peace agreement with Egypt, and he supported a bill for Israel to annex the Gaza Strip. (Annexing means that the territory would become part of Israel.) This proposal was so radical that even most Likud members failed to support it. Olmert was also against a plan that supported

an independent Palestinian state. He whole-
heartedly defended the Zionist dream of a
"Greater Israel" that included the occupied
territories and was against any peace plan that
would entail giving up this captured land.

THE OSLO ACCORDS

Meanwhile, the Palestinians, who were increasingly
fed up with Israeli occupation and the growing
number of Jewish settlements in territories that
were once theirs, began a series of revolts in the
West Bank and Gaza Strip. These revolts were
known as the First Intifada. (*Intifada* is Arabic for
"uprising.") These Palestinian campaigns included
shootings and bombings against the Israeli military
occupation.

The First Intifada didn't end until 1993,
when Yasir Arafat and Israeli prime minister
Yitzhak Rabin signed the historic Oslo Accords
in Washington, D.C., on September 13. Under
these agreements, the Palestinians, led by Arafat,
were finally allowed to partially govern themselves in the occupied territories of Gaza and

parts of the West Bank. Under the administration of an organization known as the Palestinian National Authority (PNA), Palestinians would have control over their citizens and security while the remainder of the territories, including Israeli settlements, would remain under Israeli control. In return, for the first time ever, the PLO recognized Israel's right to exist (with pre-1967 borders) in "peace and security."

The accords were meant to be the first step in the creation of an independent Palestinian state. This was a source of much dispute among many Israelis (including Olmert, who had criticized the Oslo Accords) as well as some Palestinians, who still felt that Palestine's borders would only be complete when they included the holy city of Jerusalem and all of Israel. Despite ongoing differences, in January 1996, the first Palestinian elections were held and Arafat was elected president of the new PNA.

Conflicts continued to exist, however. Israel encouraged new Jewish settlements in the West Bank. In response, the Palestinians, who had agreed to stop violence, began a new series of attacks on Israeli settlers. Citing security concerns, Israel responded by limiting the number of Palestinians who could work in Israeli-controlled territories. With most Palestinians dependent upon Israeli jobs, these new controls only helped increase poverty and fuel frustration among the Arab population.

MAYOR OF JERUSALEM

In 1993, after twenty years of serving in Israeli public office, Ehud Olmert decided to run for mayor of Jerusalem. His opponent, eighty-two-year-old Teddy Kollek of the Labor Party, had been mayor for twenty-eight years. Olmert won the election and became Jerusalem's first Likud mayor. Five years later, he was reelected for a second term.

Olmert's two terms as mayor of Israel's oldest and most religiously important city were controversial within both the country and his own family. When he took over administration of Jerusalem, it was a poor, chaotic place characterized by religious and political conflicts.

In 1999, Ehud Olmert, at the time mayor of Jerusalem, and his wife, Aliza *(center)*, join then prime minister Ehud Barak *(right)* and his wife, Nava *(left)*, during the Jewish holiday of Sukkoth.

These conflicts were inevitable since Jews, Muslims, and Christians all trace their religious roots back to this holy city. In the early 1990s, however, Jerusalem was especially difficult to govern due to the rising tensions between the city's large populations of ultra-Orthodox Jews, nonreligious citizens, and Palestinian Muslims.

Although Olmert stated in a 1997 interview with the *Middle East Quarterly* that Arabs who

Ehud Olmert, while mayor of Jerusalem, stands in front of the golden Dome of the Rock and one of the minarets (towers) on the sacred site of the Temple Mount in December 2000.

live in Jerusalem were "entitled to live on an equal basis," he also went on to say that he hoped there would "not be more Arabs living in Jerusalem." He also angered many Palestinians by encouraging Jewish settlers to build housing in East Jerusalem and by attempting to increase municipal control over Arab neighborhoods. Although he was criticized for abandoning Palestinian citizens, some claim he improved the lives of Arab residents by providing them with increased community services. Meanwhile, although Olmert had never been a religious man, his strong ties to Orthodox Jews (who had supported him during his campaign) caused droves of nonreligious citizens to move to other cities. While trying to keep the peace between all these groups, Olmert helped modernize the city. Under his administration, the city underwent a major construction frenzy; skyscrapers were built and a citywide light train system was installed.

A FAMILY DIVIDED

Olmert's most controversial and memorable act as mayor occurred in 1996. Despite warnings (including those from many friends and his wife) that he was making a mistake, Olmert, together with Likud prime minister Benjamin Netanyahu,

made the disastrous decision to reopen the
part of the Hasmonean Tunnel that led from
the holy Jewish site of the Western Wall to the
Muslim Quarter of Old Jerusalem, a sacred
area for Muslims. This ancient passage from
West (Jewish) to East (Muslim) Jerusalem had
been closed for a long time, but Olmert and
Netanyahu wanted to increase tourists' and
other visitors' access to these sites. When the
tunnel was reopened, it set off a wave of violent,
bloody riots in Jerusalem that left dead seventy
Palestinians and fifteen Israeli soldiers. Hundreds
of other people were wounded, and international
criticism was intense.

Despite Ehud Olmert's right-wing political
views, most of his and Aliza's friends were left-
wing artists and intellectuals who shared Aliza's
views. As long as they were simply arguing
about ideas, their political differences made for
lively debates. However, during Olmert's two
terms as mayor, his ideas resulted in acts that
left many of the Olmerts' friends baffled and
angry. In particular, the tragic consequences of

Police officers hold back a Muslim man who is protesting the reopening of the Hasmonean Tunnel in the Muslim neighborhood of East Jerusalem in September 1996.

Olmert's reopening the Hasmonean Tunnel so appalled several of his closest friends that they chose to break off relations with the Olmerts for many years.

Olmert's tenure as mayor created problems at home as well. Aliza Olmert also found it difficult to accept her husband's political actions, particularly his support of Jewish settlers in East Jerusalem. This period deepened the ideological differences between the couple and tested the foundations of their marriage.

The Olmert children had been educated at progressive schools, where they were encouraged to think for themselves and question authority. Ultimately, like their mother, they developed left-wing views that clashed with those of their father. For example, daughter Dana became involved in monitoring abuse of Palestinian workers at IDF checkpoints in the occupied territories. Son Ariel was a conscientious objector who refused to serve in the Israeli army. In a 2006 interview for the *Frontline* documentary "The Unexpected Candidate," Olmert jokes that in his family, he was a "minority." He goes on to say, "I always admired the tolerance of my family. . . They never got rid of me in spite of my different positions, which shows a degree of tolerance."

CHAPTER FIVE

ARIEL SHARON

In 2003, as his second term as mayor of Jerusalem was coming to an end, Ehud Olmert's old friend and Likud colleague Ariel Sharon asked him to return to national politics. At the time, Sharon had just been reelected as Israel's prime minister, and he offered Olmert the position of minister of trade and industry. Olmert wasn't tempted by the job and considered returning to his law career. However, Sharon then also promised to give him the title of senior deputy prime minister, a position that automatically would make Olmert Israel's leader if Sharon were to become ill or die. This clinched the deal, and Olmert once again became a figure in the Israeli government. In addition, he gained strength in Likud by attaching himself to Sharon's coattails.

ARIEL SHARON

Ariel Sharon was born in 1928 in a small town near Tel Aviv, in what was then the British

Protectorate of Palestine. His parents were Russian immigrants who had come to the Middle East determined to fight for a Jewish state. Barely a teenager, Sharon also became involved in the battle for an independent Jewish nation. At fourteen, he joined a Jewish military underground organization called the Haganah.

When Israel was established in 1948, Sharon was twenty. When the War of Independence broke out between Israel and its Arab neighbors, Sharon commanded an infantry group and impressed colleagues with his bravery and leadership skills. In the Six-Day War and the Yom Kippur War, he led Israeli troops to victory and became a military legend, seen by most Israelis as a national war hero.

A strong nationalist who encouraged Jewish settlements and defended the use of military force to safeguard the occupied territories, Sharon held very right-wing political views. Shortly before the Yom Kippur War, he had been one of the founders of Likud. When Menachem Begin became Israel's first Likud prime minister in 1977, Sharon was made

Israel's first Likud prime minister, Menachem Begin *(left)*, talks with his minister of agriculture, Ariel Sharon, in September 1977.

minister of agriculture. He used his position to encourage Israelis to settle in the occupied territories in order to make it difficult to return these areas to Palestinian Arabs. Obsessed since his childhood with the importance of Jews setting down permanent roots in the Promised Land, Sharon, who was nicknamed "the Great Bulldozer," succeeded in doubling the number of Jewish settlements in the West

Bank and Gaza during the four years that he was minister. Sharon therefore earned the support of many Israeli nationalists, including most of Likud. At the same time, he angered Arabs as well as Israel's left-wing citizens who hoped for peace with Palestinians.

After holding various important positions, including minister of defense, minister for trade and industry, and minister for housing construction, Sharon became leader of Likud in 1999. In 2001, he was elected prime minister. From the start, he had to deal with a serious Palestinian conflict that had begun several months before he was elected. While campaigning in Jerusalem, Sharon and an escort of several hundred policemen visited the Temple Mount complex, site of the Dome of the Rock and the al-Aqsa Mosque. Sharon infuriated Palestinians by declaring that the entire complex would always remain under Israeli control.

At the time, Israel and the PNA had been involved in an ongoing series of peace talks. However, his comments sparked a series of violent Palestinian militia revolts known as the

Ariel Sharon prays at the holy Western Wall after visiting the Temple Mount complex in East Jerusalem. His visit enraged Arab Muslim residents of the neighborhood, sparking a new Palestinian intifada.

al-Aqsa (or Second) Intifada. The violence continued for years and brought the peace negotiations to a screeching halt. In response, Sharon, now prime minister, refused to resume peace talks before Palestinians ended their campaign of suicide bombings and shootings. Although U.S. president George W. Bush tried to bring Israelis and Palestinians together to discuss a peace accord in June 2003, he was unsuccessful. However, in suggesting a "two-state solution," Bush became the first American president to support officially the creation of an independent Palestinian state. That same year, Israel began building a controversial West Bank barrier (part wall and part fence) that Sharon claimed was to prevent Palestinians from attacking Israeli citizens.

TURNAROUND

The al-Aqsa Intifada was still going strong and tensions between Israelis and Palestinians were running high at the end of 2003, when Ehud Olmert, as deputy prime minister, was asked to perform a last-minute substitution for Ariel Sharon, who had the flu. Olmert was to attend a ceremony in honor of David Ben-Gurion, Israel's founding father and first prime minister. Nobody—including politicians, the media, and Israeli citizens—imagined that anything out of the ordinary would occur at the event. In fact, barely any media attended what was expected to be a routine speech by the deputy prime minister.

However, the speech had historic significance. Olmert spoke of Ben-Gurion's dream of a "Greater Israel" that stretched from Jordan to the Mediterranean, and of a democratic Jewish state that included all the occupied territories. Then he asked which was more important, "the complete land without a Jewish state, or a Jewish state without the complete land?" He proceeded to answer his own question: "a Jewish state." A few days later, his message was heard loud and clear when he gave an interview and announced that if Israel didn't withdraw its troops and settlers from the occupied territories, it would "lead to the loss of Israel as a Jewish state." His speech shocked Likud and the entire Israeli political establishment. How could Ehud Olmert—the man who had voted against the return of Sinai to Egypt and who, as mayor of Jerusalem, had encouraged Jewish housing settlements in Muslim neighborhoods—suddenly be proposing that Israeli settlers leave the occupied territories they had fought for? Didn't this new proposal go against everything Olmert had always believed?

Throughout his political career, Olmert had never been afraid to dissent from the majority opinion. By 2003, Olmert realized that neither the Middle East nor Israel were the same as they had been years before. Realities were changing, and the situation between Israelis and Palestinians in the occupied territories was growing worse. His ten years as Jerusalem's mayor had shown him how tricky it was for Jews and Arabs to live together peacefully in the same land. As a result, his views began to change. In 2000, for example, he had surprised many colleagues when he didn't criticize then prime minister (of the Labor Party) Ehud Barak's willingness to hand over parts of East Jerusalem to Palestinians in return for a peace accord with Yasir Arafat.

However, part of his transformation probably resulted from exposure to the views of his left-wing, pro-peace friends, children, and perhaps most important, wife. "Certainly the family influenced me," confessed Olmert in *Frontline's* "The Unexpected Candidate." "I have been married to Aliza for more than thirty-five years.

So, when I finally made th[e] statement [at the ceremony for Ben-Gurion in December 2003], which really changed Israeli politics and maybe the Israeli agenda forever, my wife Aliza said, 'Thirty-five years of hard work finally bears fruit.'"

As a lawyer, Olmert had always been a practical man. In Ofra Bikel's documentary, he admitted to having changed his opinions about fundamental issues and "being proud" of these changes. In terms of Israeli relations with Palestinians in the occupied territories, Olmert explained his position in an 2006 interview published in *Moment* magazine: "'We don't want to dominate or patronize the Palestinians. . . . There has been a seismic [immense] shift in Israeli public opinion, a realization that we have to adopt practical policies that will lead to a serious peace process with the Palestinians.' And if that meant 'painful compromises,' he added, 'so be it.'"

The truth is that in the West Bank and Gaza, Palestinians heavily outnumber Jewish settlers. Combined with a growing sense that it would be impossible to reach an agreement with Arafat and the PNA, Olmert decided that Israel would on its own withdraw the 9,000 Jewish settlers who were living among the 1.3 million Palestinians in the Gaza Strip. This was the exact plan that Prime Minister Ariel Sharon officially announced to the Israelis a few days later and that, two years later, he ordered carried out.

Some Israelis believe that when Olmert made his speech for unilateral disengagement, he was testing the waters for Ariel Sharon and gauging the country's reaction. Others believe that Olmert was the one who decided upon the plan and succeeded in convincing Sharon that it was the only solution for the future of Israel. At any rate, by the end of 2003, violence and chaos had overtaken the occupied territories. Palestinian suicide bombers were regularly attacking Israeli settlers. When Yasir Arafat died in November 2004, the political instability caused by the loss of the Palestinian political leader made any further attempts at peace between Israel and Palestine even more unlikely.

Regardless of who actually came up with the disengagement plan, from August 16–30, 2005, 9,000 settlers were expelled from twenty-one

In August 2005, an Israeli settler watches a house go up in flames moments after the family living there decided to leave voluntarily their home in the southern part of the Gaza Strip.

Gaza settlements. About 14,000 Israeli soldiers and police supervised the settlers' peaceful departure. In the event of resistance, they were prepared to evacuate by force. Via television, viewers worldwide witnessed troops dragging screaming Jewish settlers from their homes and synagogues. However, while emotions ran high—even many Israeli soldiers and police were moved to tears—miraculously there was no violence.

Afterward, Israeli soldiers bulldozed all the houses. The few remaining synagogues were later looted and burned to the ground by Palestinians. The last Israeli soldier left the Gaza Strip on September 12. Ten days later, citizens and Israeli military forces pulled out from four settlements on the northern West Bank. Despite the withdrawal from the territories, however, Israel continued to control Gaza's Mediterranean coastline and airspace and to supply Gaza with water, communication, and electricity.

A majority of Israelis supported the controversial withdrawal, as did most Palestinians and Arabs, the UN, and much of the international community, including the United States. The move was viewed as coming one step closer to a final peace settlement between Israelis and Palestinians. However, Jewish settlers, Orthodox Jews, and most members of Likud were furious. They felt that the evacuation of Israeli citizens was a violation of human and divine rights since God had promised "Greater Israel" to Jews. Furthermore, they believed that removing troops would be disastrous for military security. Ultimately, members of these groups felt deeply betrayed by both Sharon and Olmert.

Olmert explained his point of view in "The Unexpected Candidate": "I don't think [the settlers] have been betrayed. I think they always knew that a large part of the population of Israel is not happy with their policy and that it may change under certain circumstances." He did, however, concede, "They may feel betrayed by people like me who once supported them and now do not."

The rift within Likud caused Sharon to leave the party in November 2005. Together with Olmert, Sharon formed a new center-left coalition party called Kadima (meaning "Forward" in Hebrew), which offered Israelis a new political alternative and chance for peace. With this development, Israel's two traditional dominant parties were marginalized, and Sharon became the first Israeli prime minister who didn't belong to either the Labor Party or Likud.

CHAPTER SIX

PRIME MINISTER

Nobody, least of all Ehud Olmert, ever imagined that 2006 would turn out to be such a momentous year for Israel, the Middle East, and for Olmert himself. Indeed, things seemed normal on the evening of January 5, when Olmert was at dinner with his wife and some American friends. However, at around 10 PM, he received a phone call informing him that Prime Minister Ariel Sharon—who was scheduled for surgery the following day—had suffered a massive stroke and was on his way to the hospital. The Olmerts soon left the restaurant and went home. Shortly thereafter, Ehud Olmert officially assumed the authority of Israel's prime minister. Ariel Sharon's situation was critical. Unconscious, he had slipped into a coma. As of early 2007, he has not awakened from it.

Aliza Olmert was completely unprepared for suddenly becoming Israel's first lady. As she recalls in "The Unexpected Candidate," "By the time we were eating dessert our home turned into a fortress. It had been covered with green cover sheets, lots of security, lots of media around it. I remember the first thing that entered my mind is that my shabby car was standing in front of the house and saying: 'Well, this is not a car of the wife of a prime minister, we should take it to the garage tomorrow.' In this country, because of security measures, everything is really so dramatic. We were following the news, and the telephones were ringing, and the red telephone was installed at home. . . . The first thing that came into my mind when we entered home was, 'Bye-bye, freedom.'"

The next day, Ehud Olmert called a cabinet meeting in which he spoke to all the ministers and announced to the Israeli public the news of Ariel Sharon's coma and that he was now acting prime minister. Olmert's televised speech, which showed him seated next to Sharon's empty chair, had an emotional impact on the Israeli public. Along with

In a televised speech in January 2006, acting prime minister Ehud Olmert sits next to the empty chair of Ariel Sharon, announcing to the public that the prime minister is in a deep coma.

mourning for Sharon, there was a great outpouring of support for Olmert. In the wake of this national tragedy, many wanted to help him settle into his new responsibilities. Olmert wasn't completely unprepared to step into his mentor's shoes. As he confessed in "The Unexpected Candidate":

"In a certain way. . . . I've been practicing for this minute all my life. . . . All my political life, I was moving forward to be in a position to take over one day." However, Olmert had never expected to become prime minister under such tragic circumstances.

HAMAS

The Olmerts, Israel, and the world at large had barely gotten over the shock of Sharon's stroke and Olmert taking over as prime minister. Yet, barely three weeks later, another unexpected, historic event threatened to change radically the situation in the Middle East. On January 25, 2006, elections were held for the Palestinian National Authority's parliament, and in a surprise victory, Hamas won the majority of government seats for the first time. Up until then, Yasir Arafat and his Fatah party had always controlled the PNA. Fatah had been considered by many to be more moderate and open to negotiations with Israel. However, Hamas is viewed by most nations (including Israel, the United States, and the European Union) as a dangerous and extremist terrorist organization, with strong links to the fundamentalist Muslim leaders of Iran. Hamas historically had been linked to violent attacks on Israeli military and civilian targets. The group had been a thorn in Yasir Arafat's side since Israeli leaders refused to negotiate for peace if Arafat was unable to control Hamas's terrorist activities. In fact, many acts of violence by Hamas members had provoked Israel into retaliating, often killing Palestinian citizens and increasing fear and anger throughout the occupied territories. Hamas had not only consistently refused to recognize all previous Palestinian agreements with Israel, such as the 1993 Oslo Accords, but had also refused to recognize Israel's right to exist.

The Hamas victory was an immense setback to any possible peace accord between Israel and the PNA. Prior to this political upset, Mahmoud Abbas, Yasir Arafat's successor as Palestinian president, had entered into peace negotiations with Sharon. Suddenly, however, all possibilities for peace between Israelis and Palestinians reached a standstill.

ELECTION CAMPAIGN

Ehud Olmert didn't plan on making peace with a Hamas-run Palestinian Authority. Since there was no sign that Ariel Sharon would come out of his coma, Olmert, along with Israel's other political parties, prepared themselves for the government elections, which already had been set for November 2005. If Olmert won, he would be legitimately elected by the people, not simply Sharon's selected replacement. As Kadima's candidate, Olmert promised to withdraw more Jewish settlements from Gaza and parts of the West Bank. He also wanted to secure Israel's borders with the Palestinians behind the steel and concrete wall that he would continue to construct.

The election, which took place on March 28, wasn't very dramatic. Most Israeli voters knew little about Olmert. In a country where 80 percent of the voting population usually turns out at the polls, almost 40 percent of them failed to vote because they were fed up with politicians.

Ehud Olmert with his wife, Aliza, after voting in the elections of March 28, 2006. Winning the election as head of Kadima, Olmert became the twelfth prime minister of Israel.

Among those who did vote, however, were the members of the Olmert family. For the first time, Aliza voted for her husband and the children voted for their father. As Aliza commented to Ofra Bikel: "I appreciate what Ehud went through and his new outlook, his new conclusions. His determination to execute [the withdrawal]. . . . I'm just sorry that it happened so late. It should have been done long ago."

On March 29, Israel's two major tabloid newspapers ran the headline "The Bang," referring to the fact that the election had shattered the structure of Israeli politics. After decades of multiparty coalitions dominated by the two ruling parties—Labor and Likud—the government was now made up of members from five major parties. Kadima had won the most seats in the Knesset, but they had won fewer seats than expected. This threatened to make Olmert's job difficult. In order to gain support for his government programs, he would have to forge alliances and a coalition with members of the other parties: the Labor Party; Shas, a Sephardi Jewish party; and Gil, a new "senior citizen" party whose main goal was to improve life for elderly Israelis. Later, he added Yisrael Beytenu, a right-wing party with a harsh view of Israeli Arabs and Palestinians, to the coalition. Relegated to the main opposition party was Likud, which after years of being in power, had suffered a humiliating defeat.

PRIME MINISTER

Ehud Olmert officially took power as Israel's twelfth prime minister on May 4, 2006. In his inaugural speech, he again spoke of his plans to withdraw settlers. He wanted Israel to become finally a "normal country," where it would be "fun" to live without the threat of a Palestinian majority in the West Bank and Gaza.

Despite the opposition expected from Likud and other ultrareligious members of government, Olmert laid out his plans: to remove some 70,000 settlers from the more remote West Bank settlements, leaving more than 400,000 settlers remaining. According to Olmert's plan, the evacuated settlers would be relocated else-where in the occupied West Bank, somewhere behind the 16-foot-high (5 meters) security wall with its barbed wire, searchlights, electronic alerts, and digital cameras. When completed, the wall would create a 475-mile-long (764 km) border separating Israelis from Palestinians.

As some political experts have pointed out, the problem with "unilateral" actions is precisely that only one party decides upon them. For Olmert's proposed new border to be recognized as a permanent frontier between Israelis and Palestinians, it must be agreed upon by Palestinians as well as Israelis. But while many Palestinians are pleased by the withdrawal of Jewish settlers, many more—including the leaders of Hamas—described the withdrawal as an

In March 2006, Palestinians walk through a metal detector at one of the many Israeli security checkpoints located in the West Bank.

affirmation of their policy of terrorism. Among Palestinians, the moderate position is that the minimum Israel should do is return all of the West Bank and Gaza back to the borders that existed prior to the Six-Day War. Another demand is to return all territories promised to the Palestinians by the United Nations in 1948, when British Palestine was split among Jews and Arabs. Hamas continues to support the elimination of Israel altogether.

Furthermore, in creating the wall, Israel will be cutting off Palestinians in the West Bank from over 200,000 Palestinians who live in East Jerusalem. This will make it very difficult for Palestinians to visit relatives, go to school and work, and simply travel from one part of their land to another. Already, Israel's military checkpoints have caused Palestinian commuters to spend hours each day waiting to pass through security checks.

NEW CONFLICTS

Ehud Olmert discovered the limits of unilateral action weeks after he took office as prime minister. Withdrawing settlers and closing the border ultimately didn't make things safer. Instead, Arab military groups provoked Israel into fighting wars in two territories it had abandoned: Gaza and southern Lebanon.

On June 25, Hamas fighters tunneled under the Gaza border into Israel, killing two Israeli soldiers and taking a third hostage. They later

Hezbollah

Hezbollah (Arabic for "party of God") is a radical Islamic military and political organization based in southern Lebanon, a small democratic nation that shares a border with Israel. The group follows a branch of Islam developed by Ayatollah Khomeini, a former leader of Iran. Its military force receives arms, training, and money from Iran. More recently, Hezbollah has also become a political party with seats in the Lebanese government. Its two main goals are to transform Lebanon into an Islamic state like Iran and to destroy Israel. Due to its frequent attacks on Israeli soldiers and civilians, Hezbollah was viewed as a dangerous terrorist organization by Israel, the United States, and Canada. However, many other countries (particularly Arab nations), view it as an armed "resistance movement" against Israel, albeit one that resorts to violent means. In fact, Hezbollah was established when Israel invaded and occupied southern Lebanon in 1982. Although Israel withdrew its troops from Lebanon in 2000, Hezbollah has continued to launch terrorist attacks on Israeli targets.

offered to trade him for some of the estimated 9,000 Palestinians in Israeli prisons. Then, on July 12, Hezbollah fighters snuck into Israel from southern Lebanon. They killed seven Israeli soldiers and took two others hostage, offering to trade them for Lebanese prisoners in Israeli jails. Considering these invasions of its borders to be acts of war, Israel quickly responded. In Gaza, Israel sent planes and tanks to destroy roads, bridges, and electrical sources, while IDF soldiers arrested a number of Hamas government officials. In Lebanon, Israeli warships closed off the harbor of the capital city of Beirut. Fighter planes blew up runways, highways, and targets in Beirut's southern suburbs, where Hezbollah has many supporters.

Unfortunately, many innocent Palestinian and Lebanese citizens were killed. Most countries around the world condemned the actions of both Hamas and Hezbollah, and admitted that Israel was provoked. However, many also criticized Israel for injuring and killing civilians, particularly in Lebanon, where Hezbollah members often hid

Israeli soldiers maneuver on top of a tank in July 2006 as Israeli missiles strike a southern Lebanese village where Hezbollah guerrilla forces are stationed.

out in residential areas. The United Nations urged all parties in Lebanon to agree to a cease-fire, which went into effect on August 14, 2006.

During the first few weeks of the war in Lebanon, Israelis rallied around the government's stance to go after Hezbollah, and Ehud Olmert's popularity ratings soared. For a while, it looked as if Olmert would establish a reputation as a tough leader like Ariel Sharon. However, when the supposedly quick and efficient air operation dragged into weeks and led to more than a hundred Israeli casualties, many people (who remembered the rapid and overwhelming victories of the Six-Day and Yom Kippur Wars) grew critical of Olmert. Many right-wing Israelis also accused Olmert of giving in to the UN's demands for a cease-fire. They believed that the IDF didn't go far enough in its attacks on Hezbollah and that the terrorist group would continue to be a threat. Some pointed out that Olmert's withdrawal and reinforcement of Israel's borders had not made Israel safer at all.

Since the end of the Israel-Lebanon conflict in August 2006, Olmert's popularity has steadily sunk. In fact, several members of the government have called for his resignation. Following the violent summer, Olmert has had to abandon his plans for unilateral withdrawal. Both Hamas and Hezbollah continue to pose threats. In Gaza, Hamas militants have fired homemade rockets into Israeli territory, leading Israeli's military to crack down on the occupied territories, including regions the government had supposedly abandoned. The Israeli government has argued that such steps are necessary for Israeli security. However, the result has led to the destruction of homes and the killing of many innocent Palestinians. Between June and November 2006, Israeli attacks killed around 300 Palestinians, 60 of whom were children. Meanwhile, between January and November 2006, Palestinian rockets killed four people in Israel. Furthermore, the existence of so many military checkpoints means that essential food, money, and medical supplies cannot circulate. As a result, the Palestinian economy has collapsed and poverty has become rampant. The fact that the international community has cut off financial aid to the Hamas government has only made matters worse. Because 70 percent of the population has no guaranteed access to food, the UN has declared the region an emergency area. The UN has also criticized Israel for punishing the Palestinian people instead of their government.

Meanwhile, conflicts are widening within the Palestinian government itself. While the PNA's

Fatah party president, Mahmoud Abbas, seeks to reopen peace negotiations with Israel, the ruling Hamas remains firm in its refusal to stop its violence or recognize Israel. Disagreements between the two groups have spread to the streets of the West Bank and Gaza, where supporters of each party routinely attack one another.

As the crisis between Israel and its Palestinian neighbors deepens, both sides will need to find a way of reaching a compromise that allows the people of both nations to live peacefully and prosperously side by side. Shortly after becoming prime minister, Olmert spoke in "The Unexpected Candidate" of being aware that Israel was going through dramatic changes and that, hopefully, they would lead to "a new beginning." Olmert went on to express his strong desire to lead his country "into new horizons, into a better future, into peace and security." Although some of his past policies have been problematic and even disastrous, he has also proved, time and time again, that he is an open-minded man, capable of surprising turnarounds and transformation.

TIMELINE

 1945 Ehud Olmert is born in Binyamina, in the British Protectorate of Palestine, on September 30.

 1947 Britain pulls its troops out of Palestine. The United Nations (UN) approves the Partition Plan to divide the land into two states, Palestine and Israel.

 1948 The UN creates the State of Israel. David Ben-Gurion becomes the first prime minister. Palestine, aided by Syria, Egypt, Jordan, Lebanon, and Iraq, attacks Israel.

 1949 The Armistice Agreements end the war between Israel and its Arab neighbors.

 1956 Israel, backed by Britain and France, invades the Sinai Peninsula.

 1963 Ehud Olmert begins his military service with the Israeli Defense Forces (IDF).

 1965 Olmert majors in philosophy and psychology at the Hebrew University in Jerusalem. He and Aliza Richter marry.

1967 On June 5, Israeli forces attack Egypt, launching the Six-Day War. On June 10, Israel agrees to a cease-fire.

 1969 Yasir Arafat becomes the leader of the Palestine Liberation Organization (PLO).

1973 Olmert is first elected to the Knesset. In the Yom Kippur War, Egypt and Syria join forces against Israel. After several weeks of fighting, Israel defeats Arab forces.

 1977 Menachem Begin is elected as Israel's first Likud prime minister.

 1978 Olmert starts his own law firm in Jerusalem.

 1979 Prime Minister Menachem Begin and President Anwar Sadat of Egypt sign a historic peace deal in Washington, D.C.

 1988 Palestinians begin local revolts—known as the First Intifada—against Israeli troops in the Gaza Strip and West Bank.

 1993 The Oslo Accords establish Palestinian self-rule under the Palestinian National Authority in the occupied territories of Gaza and the West Bank. Olmert becomes mayor of Jerusalem.

2000 Peace negotiations between Israelis and Palestinians break down when Palestinian suicide bombers attack Israeli settlers and citizens (the Second Intifada).

TIMELINE

2003 In February, Olmert becomes deputy prime minister of Israel.

2004 Longtime Palestinian leader Yasir Arafat dies.

2005 In January, Mahmoud Abbas becomes the new Palestinian leader. In August, Ariel Sharon sends troops to expel Israeli settlers living in parts of the West Bank and Gaza Strip.

2005 In November, Ariel Sharon breaks with Likud. With Olmert, he forms the Kadima party.

2006 On January 4, Ariel Sharon suffers a stroke and goes into a coma. Olmert becomes acting prime minister of Israel.

2006 On January 25, Hamas wins a landslide victory in the Palestinian elections. On March 28, Olmert is elected prime minister of Israel.

2006 Ongoing conflict in the occupied territories causes Olmert to suspend plans for withdrawal of settlers.

2007 In February, with his popularity ratings at an all-time low, Olmert meets with Palestinian leader Mahmoud Abbas and U.S. secretary of state Condoleezza Rice as part of an American attempt to restart peace talks between Israelis and Arabs.

Glossary

annex To add, attach, or incorporate territory.

anti-Semitism A hostility or hatred of Jews as a religious and racial group.

excavation An area—such as an archaeological site—in which digging is carried out.

fundamentalism Strict adherence to any set of basic ideas or principles (including religious).

Gaza Strip A heavily populated strip of Mediterranean coast, which Israel seized from Egypt in the Six-Day War of 1967. It is home to over 1.3 million Palestinians.

Hamas A militant Islamic group that is the current majority in the Palestinian government. It believes in the destruction of Israel and the establishment of an Islamic state of Palestine.

Haram al-Sharif The Arab name for the mosque complex in the heart of Jerusalem, considered to be the third most holy site in

Islam. It is also the most holy site in Judaism. Jews know it as the Temple Mount.

Hezbollah The Arab name for "party of God." Hezbollah is a radical Islamic military and political organization based in the south of Lebanon. Its goals are the destruction of Israel and to have Lebanon become an Islamic state.

intifada The Arab term for "uprising." These violent revolts erupted in the occupied territories as Palestinians protested against Israeli occupation of the West Bank and Gaza.

Irgun A radical, underground Jewish military group that operated in British Palestine during the 1930s and 1940s. Its members believed that only violence could guarantee Jews' right to a homeland.

Labor Party Israel's major left-wing Zionist party, which has been in power for a large portion of Israel's history.

left-wing Political term used to describe people or political organizations that believe in progressive and liberal ideals, including socialism and environmentalism, and that push for social change.

Likud A political coalition of Israeli right-wing and center parties (*Likud* is the Hebrew word for "consolidation"), formed in the early 1970s.

occupied territories The West Bank and Gaza Strip, seized from Jordan and Egypt respectively in the Six-Day War. Also, the eastern part of Jerusalem, including the Old City, which was subsequently illegally annexed by Israel.

Oslo Accords Peace deal negotiated between Israel and the PLO in September 1993.

Palestine Liberation Organization (PLO) The umbrella group of political and militant groups currently headed by Mahmoud Abbas. The Fatah faction is the biggest single party.

Palestinian National Authority (PNA) The interim government of the Palestinian territories, formed in 1994. (Israelis, who do not recognize a Palestinian state, always drop the "National.")

preemptive Marked by taking the initiative to act so as to lessen or eliminate another's capacity to act.

relegate To move or assign somebody or something to a less important position, category, or status.

right-wing Political term used to describe people or political organizations that support conservative, capitalistic, and/or nationalistic and religious ideas, and are against reform.

settlements Since the Six-Day War, over 200,000 Jews have populated the Gaza Strip and the West Bank, most in heavily armed colonies.

Six-Day War In June 1967, Israel fought against the Arab armies grouping on its borders. In less than a week, Israeli forces seized East Jerusalem and the West Bank from Jordan, the Golan Heights from Syria, and the Gaza Strip and Sinai Peninsula from Egypt. (Sinai was returned to Egypt in 1978.)

socialist A follower of socialism, a political theory in which the means of ownership, production, and distribution are controlled by the community as a whole.

Temple Mount The Israeli name for the site of the Second Temple in Jerusalem, the most holy place in Judaism. Arabs call the mosque complex Haram al-Sharif.

unilateral Related to or involving only one side, party, or nation.

West Bank The Jordanian territory west of the river Jordan, which Israel captured in 1967. Originally part of British-mandated Palestine, it was annexed by Jordan in 1950 after Israel's defeat of the joint Arab armies in the War of Independence.

Yom Kippur War On Yom Kippur, the most important Jewish religious holiday, in 1973, the armies of Egypt and Syria launched a surprise joint attack on Israel. After initial reverses, Israeli forces recaptured all the territory that they lost in the early days.

Zionism A Jewish political movement, which emerged in the nineteenth century, supporting a traditional homeland for the Jewish people in the Land of Israel.

For More Information

America-Israel Friendship League
U.S. National Office
134 East 39th Street
New York, NY 10016
(212) 213-8630
Web site: http://www.aifl.org

Conference of Presidents of Major American
    Jewish Organizations
633 Third Avenue
New York, NY 10017
(212) 318-6111
Web site: http://www.conferenceofpresidents.org

The Dinur Center for Research in Jewish History
The Hebrew University of Jerusalem
Mount Scopus, Rabin Building
Jerusalem, Israel 91905
Web site: http://www.dinur.org

Embassy of Israel (Canada)
50 O'Connor Street
Ottawa, ON K1P 6L2
(613) 567-6450
Web site: http://ottawa.mfa.gov.il/mfm/web/main/
    missionhome.asp?MissionID=13&

Embassy of Israel (United States)
3514 International Drive NW
Washington, DC 20008
(202) 364-5500
Web site: http://www.israelemb.org

Jerusalem Center for Public Affairs (JCPA)
Beit Milken, 13 Tel Hai Street
Jerusalem, Israel 92107
Web site: http://www.jcpa.org

The Palestine Liberation Organization
Negotiations Affairs Department
P.O. Box 4120
Ramallah, Palestine
Web site: http://www.nad-plo.org

Permanent Observer Mission of Palestine to the
  United Nations
115 East 65th Street
New York, NY 10021
(212) 288-8500
Web site: http://www.palestine-un.org

United Jewish Communities
P.O. Box 30
Old Chelsea Station
New York, NY 10113
(212) 284-6500
Web site: http://www.ujc.org

WEB SITES

Due to the changing nature of Internet links,
Rosen Publishing has developed an online list of
Web sites related to the subject of this book.
This site is updated regularly. Please use this link
to access the list:

http://www.rosenlinks.com/nm/ehol

For Further Reading

Aretha, David. *Israel in the News: Past, Present, and Future* (Middle East Nations in the News). Berkeley Heights, NJ: Enslow Publishers, Inc., 2006.

Crompton, Samuel Willard. *Ariel Sharon* (Modern World Leaders). 2nd ed. New York, NY: Chelsea House Publications, 2007.

Dubois, Jill, and Mair Rosh. *Israel: Cultures of the World.* 2nd ed. New York, NY: Benchmark Books, 2003.

Ellis, Deborah. *Three Wishes: Palestinian and Israeli Children Speak.* Toronto, ON: Groundwood Books, 2004.

Finkelstein, Norman H. *Ariel Sharon* (A&E Biography). Minneapolis, MN: Lerner Publications, 2005.

Frank, Mitch. *Understanding the Holy Land: Answering Questions About the Israeli-Palestinian Conflict.* New York, NY: Viking Children's Books, 2005.

Hayhurst, Chris. *Israel's War of Independence* (War and Conflict in the Middle East). New York, NY: Rosen Publishing, 2003.

Hintz, Martin. *Israel* (Enchantment of the World). Rev. ed. Danbury, CT: Children's Press. 2006.

Margulies, Philip, ed. *The Creation of Israel* (Turning Points in World History). Farmington Hills, MI: Greenhaven Press, 2005.

Woodward, John, ed. *Israel* (Opposing Viewpoints Series). Farmington Hills, MI: Greenhaven Press, 2005.

Bibliography

BBC News. "Profile: Ehud Olmert." January 5, 2006. Retrieved October 2006 (http://news. bbc.co.uk/2/hi/middle_east/4135680.stm).

Black, Ian. "Ehud Olmert: The Right Man at the Right Time?" *Moment*. June 2006. Retrieved October 2006 (http://www.momentmag.com/ olam/Jun06/MOM-2006-06_olmert.html).

Bowen, Jeremy. "Strategy Void Deepens Mid-East Crisis." BBC News. November 10, 2006. Retrieved November 2006 (http://news.bbc. co.uk/go/pr/fr/-/2/hi/middle_east/6136980.stm).

Butcher, Tim. "Sharon's Heir Plays Invisibility Card on the Road to Power." *Telegraph*. March 23, 2006. Retrieved October 2006 (http://www.telegraph.co.uk/news/main.jhtml? xml=/news/2006/03/23/wmid23.xml&sSheet=/ news/2006/03/23/ixworld.html).

CBC News. "In Depth: Middle East in Crisis: Ehud Olmert's Gamble." July 17, 2006.

Retrieved October 2006 (http://www.
cbc.ca/news/background/middleeast-crisis/
olmert-gamble.html).

Elon, Amos. "What Does Olmert Want?" *New
York Review of Books*, Vol. 53, No. 11, June 22,
2006. Retrieved October 2006 (http://www.
nybooks.com/articles/19105).

Erlanger, Steven. "Israeli Map Says West Bank
Posts Sit on Arab Land." *New York Times*.
November 21, 2006. Retrieved November 2006
(http://www.nytimes.com/2006/11/21/world/
middleeast/21land.html).

Gorenberg, Gershom. "Ehud Olmert: Israel's
Prime Minister Had One Epiphany. He Needs
Another." *Slate*. July 21, 2006. Retrieved
October 2006 (http://www.slate.com/id/
2146234).

The History Learning Site. "The Middle East
1917–1973." Retrieved October 2006 (http://
www.historylearningsite.co.uk/middle_east_
1917_to_1973.htm).

Keenan, Brian. "After the Flood." *Guardian*. July 22,
2006. Retrieved November 2006 (http://www.
guardian.co.uk/syria/story/0,,1826371,00.html).

Macintyre, Donald. "Ehud Olmert: The Heir
    Apparent." *The Independent*. March 25, 2006.
    Retrieved October 2006 (http://news.
    independent.co.uk/people/profiles/
    article353510.ece).

Middle East Quarterly. "Ehud Olmert: 'I Am the
    Most Privileged Jew in the Universe,'" Vol. IV,
    No. 4, December 1997. Retrieved November
    2006 (http://www.meforum.org/article/376).

Murphy, John. "Israel's Skillful Heir to Sharon."
    Baltimore Sun. March 29, 2006. Retrieved
    October 2006 (http://www.baltimoresun.
    com/news/nationworld/bal-te.olmert29mar29,
    1,3979691,print.story?coll=bal-
    nationworldutility&ctrack=1&cset=true).

O'Dwyer, Thomas. "Marriage of Inconvenience."
    Guardian. April 10, 2006. Retrieved November
    2006 (http://commentisfree.guardian.co.uk/
    thomas_odwyer/2006/04/marriage_of_
    inconvenience.html).

PBS.org. "Frontline: World: The Unexpected
    Candidate." Retrieved October 2006 (http://
    www.pbs.org/frontlineworld/stories/israel502).

Rosner, Shmuel. "Israel's Big Bang." *Slate*. March 30, 2006. Retrieved October 2006 (http://www.slate.com/id/2138944).

Taub, Gadi. "Virtually Normal: Ehud Olmert's Vision for Israel." *New Republic*. May 29, 2006. Retrieved October 2006 (http://www.tnr.com/user/nregi.mhtml?i=20060529&s=taub052906).

Weymouth, Lally. "A Conversation with Ehud Olmert." *Washington Post*. November 12, 2006. Retrieved November 2006 (http://www.washingtonpost.com/wp-dyn/content/article/2006/11/10/AR2006111001375.html).

Index

INDEX

Israeli War of Independence
(1948), 19, 64

J

Jerusalem, division of, 20
Jordan, 9, 19–20, 30, 34–35, 37,
44, 69

K

Kadima, 75, 81, 83
Kollek, Teddy, 56

L

Labor Party/Mapai, 22, 40–41,
42, 43, 51, 56, 70, 75, 82, 83
League of Nations, 9
Lebanon, 19–20, 86–90
Likud, 39–41, 47, 51, 53, 56, 59, 63,
64, 66, 69, 74, 75, 82, 83, 84

N

Netanyahu, Benjamin, 59, 60

O

Offer, Abraham, 42, 43
Olmert, Aliza (Aliza Richter), 7,
27–29, 52–53, 59, 60, 61–62,
70, 71, 76–77, 82
Olmert, Ehud
becomes acting prime minister,
4–8, 76–79
childhood and early life, 9, 18,
21, 23–24
education, 27, 39, 43

elected to the Knesset, 41
elected prime minister, 81–83
law practice, 43, 51
marriage and family, 27–29,
51–53, 59–62, 70–71, 82
as mayor of Jerusalem, 56–62
military service, 25–27, 39
Olmert, Mordechai and Bella,
14–17, 22–24
Oslo Accords, 54–55, 80
Ottoman Empire, 9

P

Palestine, history of, 9, 10–13,
17–18, 18–20
Palestine Liberation
Organization (PLO), 49, 55
Palestinian National Authority
(PNA), 55, 66, 71, 79, 80, 81,
91–92

R

Rabin, Yitzhak, 54
Resolution 242, 38

S

Sadat, Anwar, 48, 50
Sharon, Ariel, 4–8, 40, 45, 46–47,
63–68, 72, 75, 76, 77–78, 79,
80, 81, 90
Shas, 83
Six-Day War, 30–38, 39, 40, 44,
46, 49, 64, 85, 90
Suez Crisis, 25, 30, 31
Syria, 19–20, 30, 34, 35, 44–46

ABOUT THE AUTHOR

Michael A. Sommers was born in Texas and raised in Canada, Africa, and Europe. After earning a bachelor's degree in English literature at McGill University in Montreal, Canada, he went on to complete a master's degree in history and civilizations from the École des Hautes Études en Sciences Sociales, in Paris, France. For the last fifteen years, he has worked as an editor, writer, and photographer in North America, Europe, and Brazil.

PHOTO CREDITS

Cover, pp. 36, 58, 67, 82 © Getty Images; cover background Shutterstock; pp. 4-5, 85, 89 © AP/Wide World Photos; p. 10 Erich Lessing/Art Resource; p. 15 © Bettmann/Corbis; pp. 22, 41, 46, 53, 65, 77 State of Israel National Photo Collection; p. 26 © Time-Life Pictures/Getty Images; p. 33 Perry-Castañeda Library Map Collection/ University of Texas Libraries; p. 48 © Hulton-Deutsch Collection/ Corbis; p. 61 © Ricki Rosen/Corbis; p. 73 © AFP/Getty Images.

Designer: Gene Mollica;
Photo Researcher: Marty Levick